John K. Davenport, better known as "Mr. D", is the founder of Blue Rock Golf Course. Designed by Geoffry Cornish, it opened in the spring of 1962.

Mr. D, an avid golfer himself, had two hole in ones in June 1983 after sixty-five years of play. A sure proof that golf truly is an ageless game.

DEDICATION

To my grandfather, Norman P. Vickery, a golf professional
and clubmaker whose knowledge, experience, and guidance
inspired both my love for the game and the writing of
this book.

Robert V. Miller, PGA Professional

Golf
. . . the Ageless Game

John Curley & Associates, Inc.
So. Yarmouth, MA

Miller, Robert V.
Golf, the ageless game.

1. Golf.
2. Golf—Study and teaching.
3. Aged—Recreation.
I. Title.
GV965.M475 1985   796.352'3   85-7738
ISBN 0-89340-926-X

Golf—The Ageless Game
Robert V. Miller
Copyright © 1985 by
Photographs Robert M. Curley
Copyright 1985

A Special Book

Golf: The Ageless Game is more than just another golf book.

It is the first golf book published in Large Print - and there are very good reasons for that.

Large Print is easier to read, and that's good news for everybody because most people appreciate the larger type, even if their eyesight is perfect. Furthermore, in an instructional book, such as this one, the Large Print has a special advantage. You can leave the book open to any page you like, step back from it and read as you swing. In other words, you can be sure you are following instructions, and check the book against your performance, thus making sure you are practicing correctly.

As you may have surmised, the game of golf becomes more popular all the time. More people are taking up the game than ever before, and many of them are in midlife or older. We believe Large Print will be most welcome to to them, and that was one of the motives behind the publication of **Golf: The Ageless Game.** John Curley & Associates has been a pioneer in the Large Print publishing field, and with this book we invite you to discover the world of golf.

Golf is a game for all ages, as many seniors are finding out. You can look forward to many years of healthful play and - who knows - perhaps you can join those who already match their score to their age.

About the Author

Bob Miller comes from a golfing family that goes back for generations. He is an excellent golfer himself - a Class A professional in the rankings of the Professional Golfers Association. He is also a clubmaker and a professional in the repairing of clubs, a craft he learned from his grandfather.

He is also a teacher, introducing as many as 500 people per year to the world of golf. Like all good teachers, he also learns from his students, and this book reflects what he has learned over the years in the separate art of teaching golf.

Bob plays the game regularly, as head professional at Blue Rock Golf Course in South Yarmouth, and in many tournaments on his native Cape Cod. His awards tell you what kind of a golfer he is, for in the Cape Cod Pro-Am League he has been both ''Sportsman of the Year'' and ''Professional Player of the Year.''

To all who meet him, it is quickly apparent that Bob finds golf the greatest game in the world, and that imparting the joy of the game to his students is his highest satisfaction.

CONTENTS

CHAPTER

Chapter 1: Discovering Golf

Hi! I'm Bob Miller.

Welcome to the world of golf. I spend my life in that world, and I make my living at it. But I also get a great deal of **enjoyment** out of it.

My hope, with this book, is that I can help you see golf for what it really is - a **wonderful** game, a **healthy** game, a **social** game, a **fun game.** I'll be greatly fulfilled if I can show you how to get the most out of this game, the most that you want to get.

Golf is an ancient and honorable game, but its origin is shrouded in mystery. It was not invented, but rather discovered. Even Thomas Edison could not have invented a game so equally compounded of pain and joy, simplicity and aggravation, dashed hopes and fulfillment.

So the game was really discovered, perhaps, as one story goes, by the caveperson. On the way home one day from a hard day's hunting, the curved stick he was carrying accidently struck a small, round stone. The stone bounded down the trail in front of him and into an animal hole at the side of the trail. Our discoverer had just completed the world's first hole-in-one. He was overjoyed.

He pulled the stone out of the hole, backed up the trail a bit, and tried the shot again. This time he missed, of course, and therein lies the joy and pain of the game we call golf. It is a very simple game, now played around the world for fun and fitness, to shouts of joy and cries of frustration in a hundred tongues.

It is a game that touches every human emotion, is played out-of doors in beautiful surroundings, and introduces every player to other ladies and gentlemen seeking the same goals. It's a simple little game of putting a small ball in a large hole some distance away. Come, let's play. It'll do you all kinds of good!

Chapter 2: The Grip

Before you even touch the ball, you'll want to learn two very important things: Gripping the club, and addressing the ball.

The grip is perhaps the most important single element in golf. It is the connection between the club and your body. It enables you to get the "feel" of the swing, so you can control the speed and direction the clubhead travels - whether it's a good shot or a bad one.

There are three main types of grip:

1. The Overlapping grip

This is the most popular grip with men, or for anyone with medium-sized to large hands. It is easily formed by placing the top of the club handle into the palm of the left hand (for right-handers). Then cover the left hand with the right hand, overlapping the right pinkie into the valley between the first and second fingers of the left hand. Now close the hands comfortably around the shaft-top.

Apply enough pressure so that you have a firm grip on the club but are not trying to strangle it. You don't want the club to turn in your hands, neither do you want it frozen. Remember, your hands are going to transmit the "feel" of the club, so that you come to "feel" the difference between a good, sound shot and one that is too "soft" or too "hard."

2. The Interlocking Grip
This grip is often used by men, and frequently gives women a feeling of more security. It is formed the same as the overlap, except that the right pinkie is actually hooked between the first and second

fingers of the right hand (see illustration). The hands are now physically linked and work as a pair to transmit "feel."

3. The Baseball Grip

This is a ten-finger grip with no joining of the fingers. It looks and feels very much like grasping a baseball bat and is most often used by juniors or persons with small hands. It is frequently the most comfortable grip for anyone with arthritis.

The choice of grip usually depends on:

(a) Comfort - which feels best for you,

(b) Size of hands - small, medium or large,

(c) Disabilities - The grip can be adapted to accommodate many types of hand or arm problems so that you can enjoy the game of golf. Consult your professional to help develop the grip best suited to you.

12

4. Forming the Grip

First place the club in the last three fingers of the left hand, about one-half inch below the end of the grip. (See illustration.) Close the palm of your left hand on the club. Turn your hand slightly to your right, so that the V formed between the thumb and first finger points toward your right shoulder - Place your right hand on the grip, below the left hand, and form the grip of your choice (see above). The center of the right palm should rest on top of the left thumb. The middle two fingers of the right hand wrap around the grip to secure it, while the index finger wraps around to touch the right thumb. This forms another V between the right index finger and thumb, and this V should also point to the right shoulder.

Try this exercise (illustrated).

Drop arms to side and form semi-fists.

Keep arms extended and move them up in front of face.

13

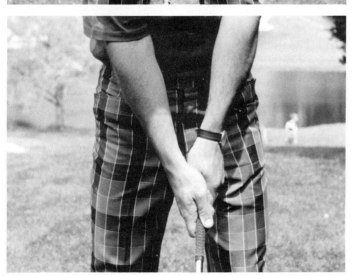

Notice the Vs pointing to your right shoulder.

Conclusion: A natural position.

Grip pressure:

How hard can you squeeze an egg before it breaks? Not very hard. In golf, too tight a grip builds up tension and rigidity throughout your body. Relaxing your hands a bit, and your arms and upper body keeps you free of tension, makes for an easier, more effective swing.

You can practice your grip constantly, and you should. You can do it indoors at any-time, year-round. If possible, check your grip in a mirror. Do it until you "feel" perfectly comfortable with your grip. Remember that your grip is the most important pre-swing fundamental, and that a good grip gives you more accuracy and more distance. It helps to keep you in a fairway, and get those precious extra yards.

Chapter 3: ADDRESSING THE BALL

To begin the swing correctly, you must first stand up to the ball correctly. This is called addressing the ball.

The most common shot for all golfers is the drive off the first tee and it is usually a wood shot. So let's take a look first at the basic stance for the wood shot, off the tee - that raised, grassy mound at the start of each hole.

This basic stance - as adapted and refined to suit your needs - will serve you throughout your game.

1. Wherever your ball lies - on the tee, in the fairway, or in the rough - step behind it and look ahead at the target - where you want the ball to go. Make a mental picture of it, and keep the picture in mind.

2. Walk around the side of the ball, so your body is at right angles to the path of the flight. Step up towards the ball.

3. Face the ball with feet slightly apart - about the width of your shoulders. Your body should be at right angles to the line of flight. Take a square comfortable stance, with your weight directly over your feet. Your right foot should be squarely perpendicular to the target, the left foot toed slightly toward the target, say 10 to 15 degrees. Ball position center of your stance with irons, and inside the left heel with wood shots.

4. Distribute your weight evenly on both feet. Think of the center of your body being where your Adam's apple is. That is the center of your swing arc, and you want to keep that pointed steadily at the ball, regardless of how the rest of your body swings.

5. Flex your knees slightly. This frees up the lower body and leg action.

6. Let your arms hang comfortably in front of your body. Grip your club and place the club head behind the ball. Move far enough away so that your arms and club shaft go straight to the ball. This will depend on the length of your

arms and of your clubs. Your distance from the ball should be comfortable - not too far away, not too close. With experience, and the help of your professional, you will soon learn the distance that is proper for you. You can then address the ball firmly, confidently, and comfortably.

7. Keep your head steady, but not rigid. Focus your eyes just behind the ball. Think of your Adam's apple as the center of your swing. Everything revolves around that center.

8. As you set up, your left arm and club shaft should make a straight line with your hands falling just inside your left knee. The right arm will be relaxed and folded in toward your right hip.

You are now ready for the swing, but first let's take a look at some of the most interesting - and frustrating - strokes in golf: putting, chipping and pitching.

Address position with irons.

Chapter 4: PUTTING

Putting is the stroke that makes all players equal, and the putter is the most used club in the bag. As one aphorism has it, ''Drive for show and putt for dough.'' Putting can count for up to 40 or 50 percent of your score, and skill at putting can give you back a lot of bad shots accumulated on the way to the green. Here's how to get the best out of putting:

1. Approach the putt positively and with confidence. A great part of putting is nerve; if you are not ''in charge,'' nobody is. The proper mental ''set'' gives you a better chance to drop that ball in the cup, be it a piddling putt or a 60-footer.

2. The grip. The reverse overlap (see illustration) is the most popular on the tour today. You can use that, or any of the three basic grips described in Chapter 2, or fashion your own grip. You'll see many a strange grip among our fellow players; the main thing is to develop the grip that works for you.

What matters is how many putts you sink, or don't sink!

3. The address. A square stance, feet evenly across, spread at shoulder width, works best for most people. Flex the knees, and bend from the waist, with the ball forward and just inside the left heel. Think of parallel lines (see illustration), one across the toes just left of the target, the other running from the ball right through the target.

4. The eyes should be directly over the ball. If you dropped a ball from your eyes it would land on the ball you are addressing.

5. Your arms should form an upside-down triangle, your shoulders forming the base, your hands the apex where they meet at the club.

Early this past season my putting game had what I call "the edges." The ball kept spinning off the side of the hole. My putts were close, but weren't dropping in.

One afternoon while on the Practice Green I realized I was visualizing a "narrow thread" line to the cup instead of a

wider path of about four inches. This is about the width of the cup and it gives the putter two inches on either side of the center of the hole. I found that giving myself this wider path removed the pressure and by relaxing the putter in my hands I was sinking many more putts than before. Of course sinking more putts reduces your score considerably!

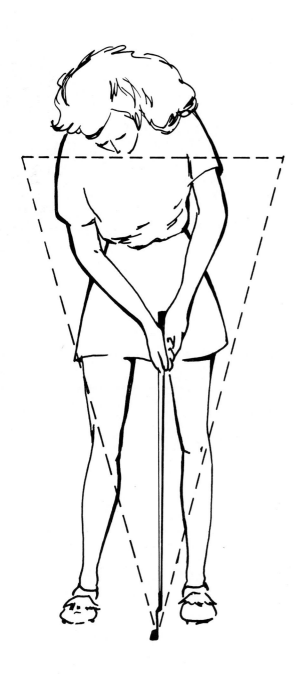

6. The Stroke. The triangle moves back and forth at equal distance like a pendulum.* There is no break of the wrists; your shoulders and arms control the swing of the penddulum. The clubhead stays square to the ball and close to the ground. Accelerate the clubhead evenly through the stroke, and control distance by shortening or lengthening the distance the clubhead travels. As a rule of thumb, the ball will travel one foot for each inch the clubhead goes back. Watching the putter strike the ball will help you stay steadier over the ball, especially on those two-foot putts.

7. The short putt. Start with some two- or three-footers to build your confidence and positive attitude. Get the feel of the putter making solid contact with the ball, and watch the ball rolling toward the cup. Before you even strike the ball, visualize it dropping in the hole. Think: ''I can make this putt. I can make it.''

Address and check alignment

Address Position

The Putting Stroke

8. The long putt. I call a long putt 15 feet or more. Basically the only difference between that and a short putt is the length of your stroke. Estimating the distance is the problem for most golfers. You'll see the pros look at the shot from the back, hold the putter up and look through the shaft - many a pet exercise. One of the best ways to estimate distance is simply to walk about halfway to the cup and look back at the ball. This gives many golfers a good estimate and "feel" for the distance.

Another tip: Think of a three-foot circle around the hole, or imagine the hole as a bushel basket. This gives you a bigger target, and a better chance of getting inside it. Remember that if you can come within three feet of the hole on a long put, the odds are in your favor to make a good putting score. Outside of that circle, the odds begin to dwindle fast. Don't worry about one-putting on those long ones; you'll get your share of those. The main thing is to avoid more than two putts per hole. Those extra putts can quickly zoom your score.

9. The breaking putt. This is one of the toughest shots in the game, and here's where your positive attitude comes in. Every player has to make these shots, and you can make your share - and maybe a little more - if you study the problems and practice the solutions. Most greens are not level, even if they look like they were. The undulate, and it is these slopes, valleys and hills you have to "read" so you can conquer them.

Start to "read" your green as you come in on your approach shot. Watch what happens to your ball after it hits the green, and watch what happens with your fellow player's ball. Watch the putts that come ahead of yours. In other words, go to school on the other fellow; see what the problems are and how he solves them, or fails to.

Once on the green, the best way to size up your shot is to crouch behind the ball and look closely at the track your ball will have to follow to the cup. If the green is not entirely level (and it rarely is) your ball is going to "break" one way or the other as it negotiates those hills and slants of the ground.

You have to calculate those breaks so that the ball will curve back onto track and go in the cup. There's no substitute for experience on this, but here are a few tips.

Direction. In the breaking putt pick a spot at the height of the curve that is either left or right of the target. Aim your ball at that spot by facing the label of your ball at it. Center the putter's sweet spot on the label and you are aligned to get break on your ball.

Speed. Now you want to get enough speed for the ball to hold the line to the hole. Here you should use what is called the "pro side" - giving your ball the right break and enough speed so it has a chance to go in. The amateur side is when you don't achieve the right break or the ball ends short or below the hole. Rule of thumb: The harder the ball is hit the less it will break, the softer the more break. Watch your ball when it goes by the hole, because it will break the opposite way coming back.

Breaking putts are hard, but nothing gives more pleasure than when you start to master them.

10. Hillside putts. On downhill putts, picture the cup as closer to you than it really is. In other words, on a 10-footer, think of it as an 8-footer. On a severe downhill, hit the ball on the toe of your putter.

The ball will come off much slower, preventing overshooting. On the uphill putt, picture the hole as farther away and hit the ball dead center.

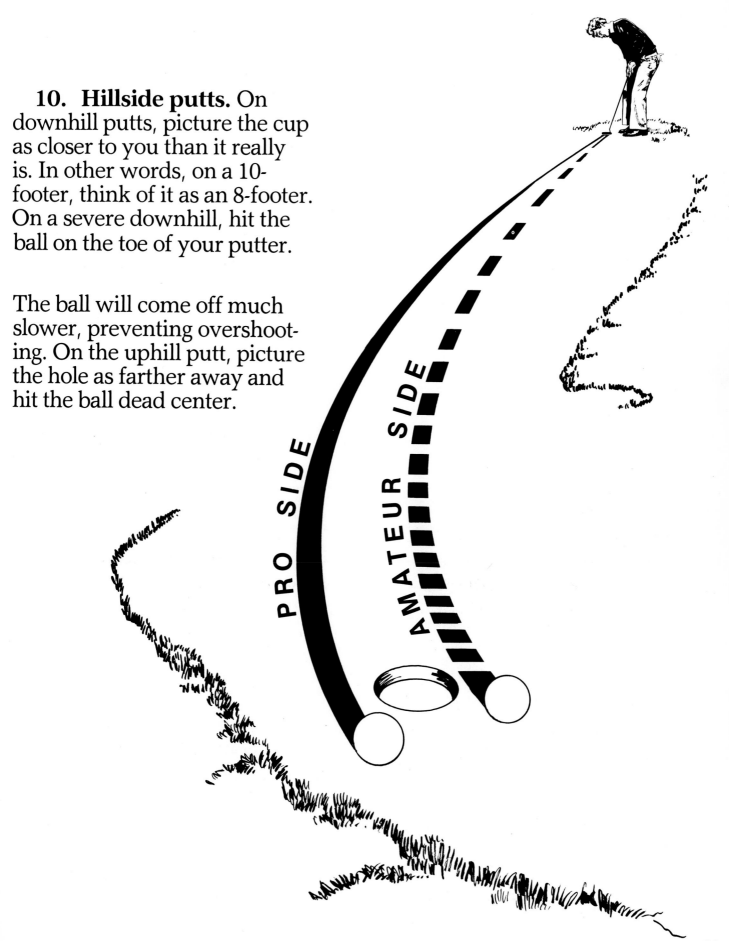

PRO SIDE

AMATEUR SIDE

11. Choosing the right putter. They come in some pretty weird sizes and shapes, giving you a chance to express your personality, but its probably best to start off with a more-or-less standard club. Try out several putters at your pro shop, and choose one that looks and feels good. Choose one with a line, or dot, at the so-called "sweet spot." As you get more into the game, you may find a new putter can change your whole outlook. So get another one; most players own more than one putter. Strike your blow for individuality.

12. Putting Drills

(a) Keep track on your scorecard of how many putts you take on each hole. Two putts per hole is a good goal to shoot for. Most tour players average 29 or 30 putts per round.

(b) Try putting contests with friends on the practice green. This will give you a sense of competition and simulate actual play, where you only get one chance.

(c) Practice your stroke between two parallel 2 x 4s. Number them on one side in the center with 0 then one inch apart 1, 2, 3, 4, 5, 6, 7, 8, 9, 10,

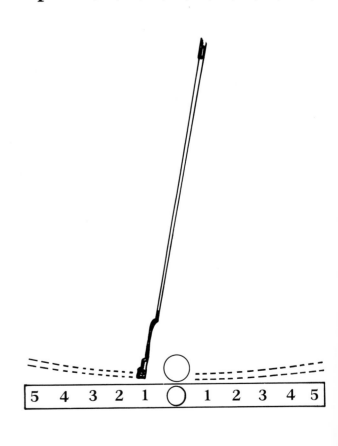

then 10, 9, 8, 7, 6, 5, 4, 3, 2, 1. The timbers will help you get a straight back, straight through swing, and the one-inch-equals-one-foot rule will develop your pendulum stroke.

(d) Put several balls around the cup three feet away and putt those three-footers from all directions. They are the scoring putts you want to make.

(e) Practice long putts by putting tees in a two-foot circle around the cup. Then try to get those long putts within the zone. Try all distances from 15 feet to 50 feet to gain confidence with long putts.

(f) On breaking putts, put a tee at the height of the break and then try to gauge the speed needed to achieve the correct amount of break. Another good drill is to lay a string down along the intended line and try to see how close you can follow the string.

(g) If you are having a problem keeping the wrists firm use a sweatband around the putter and wrist to hold the putter securely in place to prevent unneeded movement.

(h) Indoor practice is good, especially in winter, to keep the "feel" and a confident stroke going year-round.

Putting from the Fringe
The first cut off the green is referred to as the fringe. It is usually three or four-feet wide. Whenever you can, use your putter from the fringe. The success ratio is higher with the putter than a lofted iron. Just add an inch to the putting stroke.

Chapter 5: CHIPPING

The chip shot is used to put the ball on the green when it lies only a short distance - 10 yards or so - from the green. The pendulum stroke is used in chipping, the same stroke we employ for putting. Club selection. depends on your lie - whether you are in the rough, on the fringe, or in the fairway.

First take a good look at the flag stick on the green and study the green for those hills and valleys. How much distance is there between the edge of the green and the flag? This is a key factor, since it determines how much roll we want on the ball after it hits the green. Too much roll or too little determines how close to the pin your ball will stop.

If the stick is close to the edge of the green - less than 20 feet - use a club with more loft, say a 9 iron. If the stick is **very** close to the edge, you can use a pitching or even a sand wedge. Remember that on chip shots your ball should be in the air about two-thirds of the distance to the pin, with a one-third roll on the green.

When your ball lies 30 to 45 feet from the pin, you can use a 7 iron, and for 60 feet or more try the 5 iron. On these chip shots your ball should be ⅓ in the air and ⅔'s roll. In all chipping shots the stroke is the same but the loft on the clubface determines the distance the ball will travel in the air and how far it will roll.

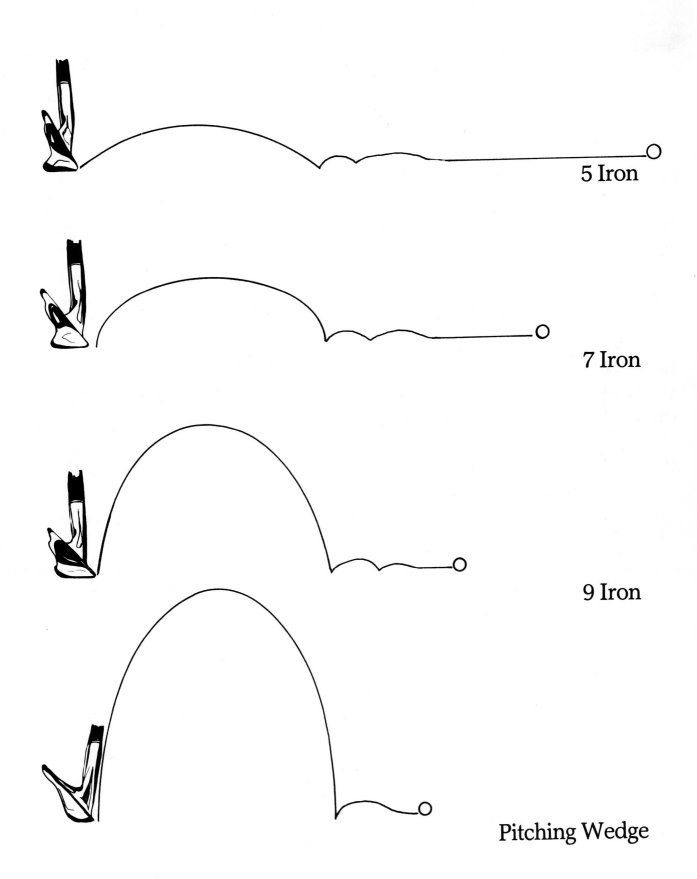

5 Iron

7 Iron

9 Iron

Pitching Wedge

Addressing the ball.

Addressing the Ball

For chip shots, choke up on your club - that is, move your grip down an inch or two from the normal position on the club handle. This will give you better control over the chip. Open your stance by dropping your left foot back 4 or 5 inches from the right foot. Keep your feet about a foot apart.

Place most of your weight on the forward part of your left foot, flex your knees, and bend from the waist toward the ball. Now form the pendulum - or upside down triangle - with your arms and club, the same as in putting. Your hands should be set slightly ahead of the ball, and just inside the left knee, with the ball in the center of your stance.

Swing back to 8 o'clock.

Follow through to 4 o'clock.

On the eighteenth hole during a tournament I had a good round going, until I missed the green on a short par 3. My ball landed about three yards or so to the right of the green. Because of a bad lie and only about twenty feet of green to work with, I had a problem. The greens that day were extremely fast and this one sloped away from me. A sand wedge was the club to use as the ball needed only a four yard flight and a fifteen foot roll. With firm wrists and soft hands

I gently chopped the club down behind the ball. It popped up and slowly ran down the slope stopping two and a half feet below the hole. Yes, the putt went in too!

Chips from the Deep Rough

Club selection is the key. Use a sand wedge from deep grass. It has higher loft to get your ball up and out, and stop it quickly. The sand wedge is heavier and with more weight on the bottom of the club, thus it glides through deep grass easier than with a lighter and less lofted club.

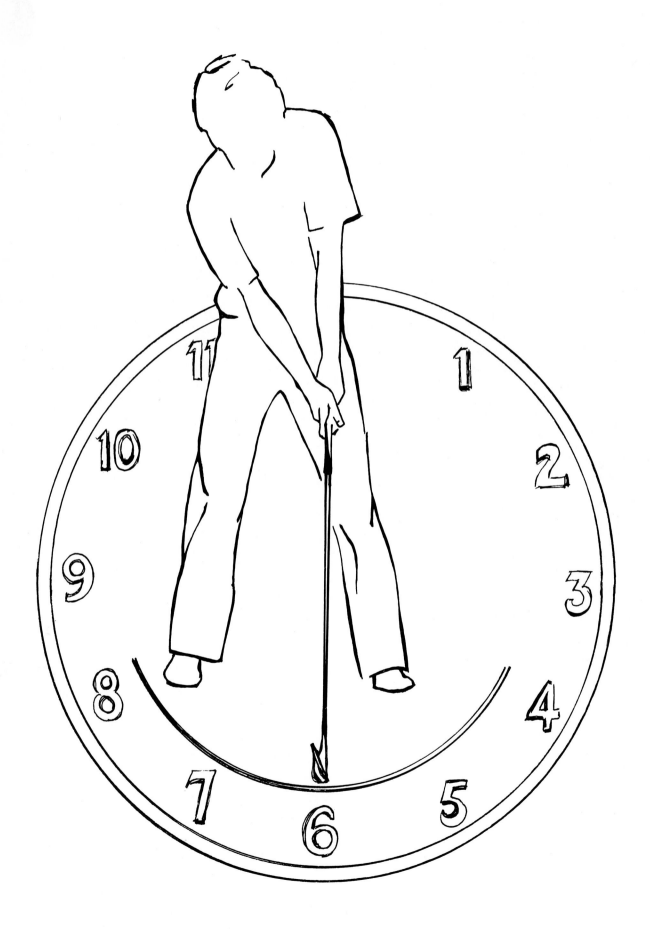

As you swing, think of hitting the grass under the ball. Getting the ball up into the air is a matter of the clubhead descending downwards on the ball. As you swing through, the ball will rise, as you want it to do.

The Stroke

Use the pendulum swing, keeping your wrists firm and swinging from the shoulders, an equal distance backwards and forwards. Hit the whole ball crisply, and brush the grass under it to loft the shot. Think of a clock face, and swing your club mostly from eight to four. Accelerate the stroke through the ball, and do not quit upon impact. Keep the knees flexed during the entire shot. Lifting up will cause you to top the ball.

Always finish the stroke with the clubhead on the line of target.

Just as in putting, a good study of the green will pay off. Find the spot on the green where you want the ball to land, so that it will break and roll properly toward the cup.

Drills

1. Practice frequently with different irons and become familiar with the distances your ball rolls once it hits the green.

2. Circle the flag stick with tees in a three- to four-foot circle and see how many balls you can chip within the zone.

3. Using ten balls chip, and then putt. Keep track of your percentage in getting the ball down in two shots, one chip and one putt.

Chapter 6: THE PITCH SHOT

This is also called the approach shot, and is really a long chip shot. Use it when you are 50 yards or less from the green. Just as in the chip shot, you should study the green, and the contours of the green's surface, so you get the right break and run on the ball.

The Address Position
1. Open the stance slightly,
2. Ball position again in the center of the stance,
3. Knees flexed,
4. Weight favoring left foot,
5. Club selection is determined by the distance you have from the edge of the green to the flag stick. If the stick is forward of the center of the green, use a pitching wedge or 9 iron. If the stick is in the center of the green or on the back, use a 7 iron.

Think about how much you want the ball to roll. Use a lofted club when pitching over bunkers.

Pitching Experience
The tenth hole at my course has a steeply faced bunker to the right, and short of the green. With the pin cut on the right side of that bunker, you are indeed confronted with a most difficult shot.

Pick a spot at the flagstick or beyond. Select a pitch or sand wedge.

Take a little longer swing to get both the distance and height required.

When you are able to get a shot like this one close to the stick it will make other pitch shots seem relatively "easy".

Address Position

The Stroke

1. Think again of the numbers on the face of a clock. With your head positioned at twelve swing the club from nine to three o'clock, or from waist-high on your body.

2. Swing from the shoulders and forearms. Wrists remain firm again.

3. In this stroke let your flexed knees flow towards the target, and shift your weight slightly left to gain a little more distance. The clubhead passes downward through the ball to add loft.

4. Finish with the clubhead pointing at the flag stick.

5. Picture trying to get the ball within a six- to eight-foot circle.

Hands Back to Waist High

Follow Through to Waist High

33

Chapter 7: THE FULL SWING

It certainly looks beautiful, doesn't it, when Nancy Lopez or Jack Nicklaus steps up there and whams that ball 200 yards or better straight down the fairway. And it looks so easy! Wow, if only I could swing that way! Well, you can. You can learn to swing sweet enough to get a good drive off the tee, put the ball on the green with a couple of good approach shots, and sink that putt for a respectable score. Taking the ball from tee to green is all a matter of swing, the same basic swing for all clubs; it's just a matter of learning a free and easy swing - one that you are comfortable with - and modifying it to the circumstances all the way down the fairway to the green. Let's start working on it.

The full swing is the one that takes you off the tee, where everybody is watching you and you get more nervous by the minute. Relax! This is a game, remember! You're supposed to be enjoying yourself. Think of rule No. 1: Don't try to kill the ball. What you want is a respectable shot down the fairway. If you keep the ball straight, out of the rough on either side, don't worry about distance. Distance will come along in good time, as you smooth out your swing and get more power behind it. Right now let's try for a good, smooth swing.

The Backswing
The backswing is the wind up, where you gather up the energy you will release at impact.

1. Begin the backswing by pushing the club backward away from the ball in a straight line for about a foot, using your left hand and arm.

2. In the same manner, keep the club going back until you reach waist-high, as in the pitch shot.

3. The goal of the back-swing is to create a long arc which results in more distance. As you take the club back, you form a long straight line from your left shoulder to the club back, you form a long straight line from your left shoulder to the head of your club.

4. As the club continues back from waist-high the shoulders turn away from the ball like turning to shake hands with someone. This produces a coiling action in the upper body.

5. The right elbow remains close to the side or right hip and folds out of the way.

6. As the club swings past waist-high the wrists begin to hinge, which now adds a lever to the golf swing.

7. Upon reaching the top of the backswing the hands should be at least shoulder height and with the wrists fully hinged.

8. The length of the back-swing adds flexibility to your body. The more flexible you are the easier it is to swing the club back to the top of the backswing.

9. As the club swings back, 60 to 70 percent of your weight shifts to the inside of the right foot as you reach the top of the backswing. This is done by just rocking the left foot to the right and the left knee to the right. The middle of your body remains over the ball.

10. The last three fingers of the left hand should be secure, holding the club steady. This prevents the grip from coming loose and changing the direction of the club on the down-swing.

11. At the top of the back-swing your club should be parallel with the ground, with the clubhead pointing at the target.

The Downswing

The downswing returns the clubhead to the ball, releasing the stored-up energy created during the backswing.

1. The downswing begins when your weight begins to shift from the inside of the right foot over to the left foot. This is done by turning the right knee towards the left knee.

2. Immediately pull down on the club with the left hand and side to return the club to the impact zone. During the descent, the right elbow brushes by the right hip.

3. When the clubhead is within three or four feet of the ball the wrists begin to unhinge, or straighten out. This increases the speed of the clubhead.

4. At impact, the clubhead reaches maximum velocity and the wrists return to a straight line. The clubhead should accelerate evenly from start to impact.

5. Throughout the backswing and the downswing, your one thought is to meet the ball squarely with the clubhead and keep your shot in the fairway. Don't try to kill the ball. Swing your club at about 80% of your full power. This will give you more control and better drives. Remember that accuracy is a premium in golf. It is easier to play off the fairway than from the rough rough or woods.

The Follow Through

1. At impact, a complete transmission of energy has been imparted to the ball.

2. A millisecond after impact the right hand and arm cross over the left. This is referred to as the release of the swing and club.

3. The arms continue toward the target, much as in the finish of the pitch shot.

4. Continue your hands and arms until they reach maximum length, finishing high above and opposite the left side of the head.

5. The lateral weight shift is completed when your right knee is pointing at the target and is nearly touching the left knee. Most of your weight will be on the left foot, and only 10 to 20 percent on the right toe. Your buckle should be pointing at the target. A good flowing weight shift and a wide and long swing arc will help increase your distance and control.

The intention of all golfers whether conscious or unconscious is to hit the ball as far as they can, especially on the tee shot. While qualifying for the 1982 "National Long Drive" contest at Brewster Golf Club on the Cape with my young assistant I had an unforgettable experience. His name was Kevin Carey, a lefthander, who is today the longest driver of the ball I have ever seen. Two players would be qualifers and would move on to the sectional contest. The fairway was forty yards wide with a cross wind quartering over my right shoulder. My first drive split the fairway and was marked at 296 yards. The next was in the middle about 285 yards, and next I hit a bullet that caught a good bounce which finished at 319 yards. From that shot on, Kevin and I had a duel, but as we each swung harder and harder we rarely kept the ball within the forty yard markers to have the drive count. Our percentage of balls in the fairway was only about one out of five. Kevin crushed one ball an incredible 339 yards to finish first, I was second. We both moved on to the sectional meet; Kevin finished in fourth place, and I at tenth place in New England.

After those two contests it took me a month to get my tempo back on my tee shots as I was still trying to "kill the ball". I finally took out a ladies driver with a ladies flex shaft and just tried to meet the ball with half of my strength; at last the groove came back! Since that time I have skipped the Driving Contest. It ruined my tempo causing my entire game to suffer.

Chapter 8: PRE-SHOT ROUTINE

It is a good to develop a pre-shot routine, a series of movements before you take your stroke. Each player has a little different approach, and repeating it leads to more consistent play. Here's my pre-shot routine:

1. Get directly behind the ball and visualize the flag stick or target line and the flight of the ball.
2. Walk up to the side of the ball and step into your stance with the right foot, planting it squarely.
3. Grip the club.
4. Put the club behind the ball and aim the face at the target.
5. Bring the left foot into the stance.
6. Look at the target while waggling the club to relax.
7. Get a positive thought and begin your swing.

Developing a routine makes you approach the ball exactly the same way each time, and helps you to improve your grip and address. It is helpful from tee shot right through putting. Try it!

Consistency begins with the Pre-Shot Routine. At a golf tournament some years ago I realized during the round that I didn't approach my golf shot the same way each time. I approached the ball from the side or from the back, or sometimes by just waling up to it with no vision of the shot in mind. After developing a mental check-list my pre-shot routine began to show me the shot clearly.

Visualize The Shot

Step In With Right Foot

Assume Address Position

Point Your Belt Buckle at the Target

Chapter 9: IRON PLAY

The irons have more loft than the woods, and the shafts are shorter. Most players have better control with the irons, which means better accuracy in laying the ball onto the green. With more loft, you can lift the ball out of bad lies and take it over traps and other hazards to the green. The irons can also be used off the tee on short holes. Now let's look at the main groups of irons.

The Short Irons

1. There are the pitching wedge and the nine, eight and seven irons. They are most often used when hitting to the green from 125 yards or less, depending on the power of your swing and the conditions on the course. Position the ball in the center of the stance.

2. All shots are hit on the downswing, to create backspin and hold the green. You've seen the golf ball on TV hit the green and back up? That's backspin.

3. The more lofted irons are used when traveling over bunkers or other hazards surrounding a green. The higher trajectory of these clubs gives less distance but improves accuracy and produces softer landing shots, with less roll.

4. Keep a good, even tempo with these lofted irons and they will hit a lot of greens for you.

The Middle Irons

1. The four, five and six irons are referred to as the middle irons.

2. Distances are usually from 135 to 165 yards.

3. Use the same swing as with the short irons but with the longer shaft and less loft the ball will have a lower trajectory. You get more distance and more roll with these clubs.

Blue Rock Golf Course is one of the finest and most challenging Par Three Courses in New England, and I have been its Head Golf Professional for seven years. Here you have what I call a "Championship Course" without tee shots. Your irons are used off the tees on most holes as they require more accuracy than regular tee shots. The iron game is one of correct distance and accuracy rather than how far you hit the ball.

One day on our seventeenth hold, measuring 135 yards we held a "hit the green" contest. The pin was cut about in the center of the green and a soft wind was in the player's face. The object was to hit the green and win a prize. With more than one hundred players only about ten percent hit the green. Most of the players missed the green or were short. They were not taking into consideration that the wind would knock the ball down and thus were under clubbing themselves.

Take the club that will comfortably get you to the center of the green, not a club that requires you to hit your Sunday best to get you there. How many players ever fly the green in the air?

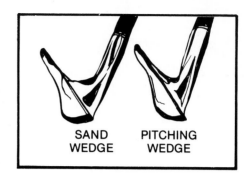

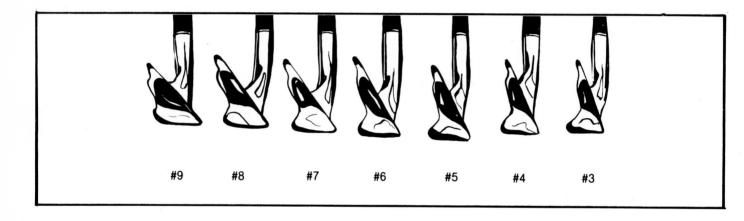

#9   #8   #7   #6   #5   #4   #3

The Long Irons

1. The one, two and three irons are the long irons, and they are the most difficult to hit. I suggest using only the three iron for a while, because with the less loft it is harder to get the ball airborne. It requires strong downward action to get the one and two irons on a high enough trajectory to gain any distance. These irons have lower trajectories and roll considerably. They are often used by professionals on tight holes requiring good accuracy.

The three iron is a good club to keep the ball low when coming out from under trees.

2. The three iron is good for 165 to 170 yards when well struck.

Key Point

Keep track of the different distances your iron shots travel. You will probably find there is about ten yards or so between clubs. So when you size up your next shot, figure your yardage and pick the right iron for the job.

Addressing a Wood

Chapter 10: WOOD PLAY

Wood play is broken into two categories: tee shots and fairway shots. Each uses the same swing and method, but the big difference is club selection.

The woods are less lofted than the irons and the shafts are longer, resulting in greater and more powerful swing.

They are distance clubs, but the farther the ball travels the less the accuracy. We begin almost every hole with a wood shot and use them for a lot of second shots. Keep them under control. Resist that natural impulse to ''kill'' the ball.

The basic change for woods is the ball position. The ball with all woods is played left of center in the stance, in line with the left heel.

The Tee Shot
1. The most frequently used wood for the tee shot is the driver of No. 1 wood. It is the most difficult club in the bag to control.
2. Tee it up high enough. Half of the ball should be above the top of the clubhead.
3. The swing with a driver is like that of any other club, but the tendency is to over-swing. Don't loose control by letting the grip go at the top of the swing.
4. The swing path is that of a sweeping action, downward through the ball, causing it to

assume a low trajectory. The lower trajectory produces more roll and cuts the wind.

5. Evenly accelerate the driver through the swing, with a good weight transfer and solid contact. This will produce straighter and longer tee shots.

6. Use a three wood off the tee if:

(a) you have a following wind. This will give you a higher and longer ball flight.

(b) you want more accuracy. A driver may go farther but a three wood will keep you in the fairway more often.

Fairway Woods

The fairway woods are used when the green is beyond the range of the irons. These shots occur most often on the long holes, par four or five. They are the distance clubs from the fairway.

I recommend more lofted woods from the fairway, such as a five or seven wood. Only try the three wood when you have an excellent lie.

Remember, you must get the ball airborne to achieve distance.

1. Ball position is forward opposite the left heel, and strike the ball on the down-swing.

2. If you are having trouble getting the ball up use a more lofted wood and actually try to hit a divot while striking the ball.

3. A high loft wood may also be used from a shallow fairway bunker.

4. Use a seven wood when trying for distance from the rough off the fairway.

5. The set of woods should contain a driver, and the 3,5, and 7. There are a variety of high loft woods available, similar in loft to a seven wood. Try them out and see if they work for you.

First, address the ball with confidence, as discussed in Chapter 3. Settle into position and you are ready for the swing.

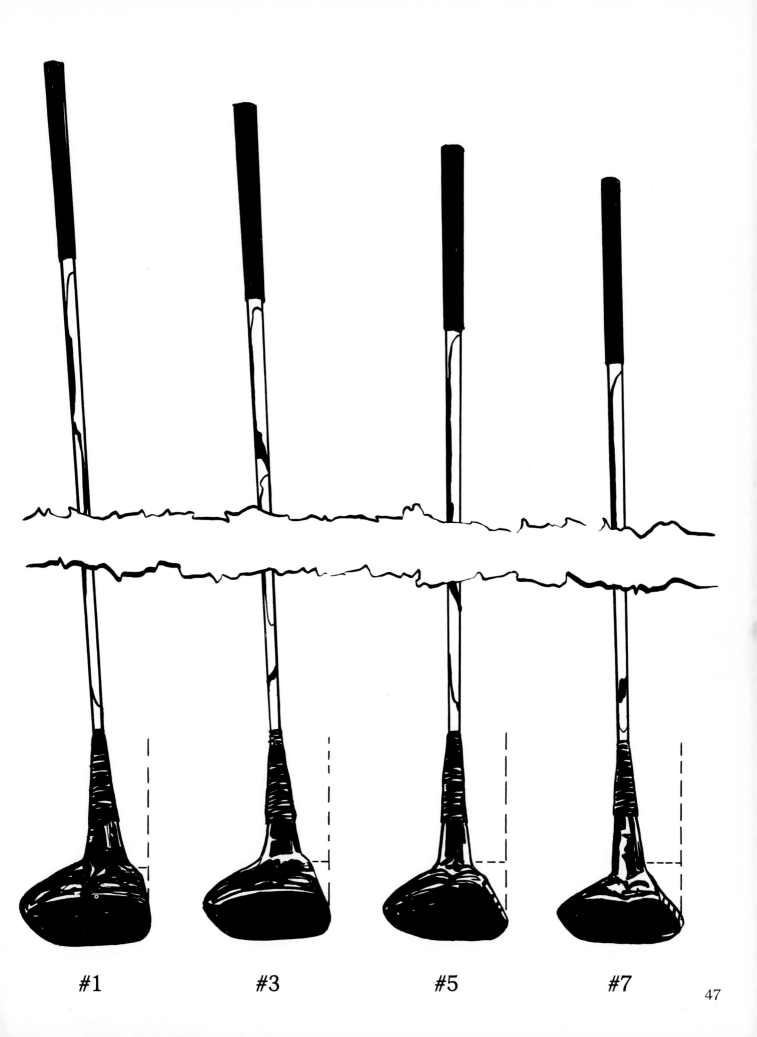

#1   #3   #5   #7

Chapter 11: Hazard Shots

There are two types of hazards on the golf course-the bunker or sand trap, and the water hole. Water holes are really a mental hazard, and we'll discuss them a little later. The sand trap is a physical hazard - once your ball goes in, you have to get it out. There is also a very strict rule in golf - in the sand trap your club can touch the ground only once, when you actually strike the ball. In your address and your practice swings, you must keep the clubhead from touching the sand; a touch can cost you a two-stroke penalty. Sand traps usually guard the green, but also used on some fairways, just to make your shots a little more difficult. Here's how to handle traps:

Backswing to Shoulder Height

Hit the Sand Behind the Ball

You Must Follow Through

The bunker shot is one of the most feared and probably the least practiced of all golf shots. When I have a practice session I begin my workout in the bunker so as not to overlook or forget this important shot.

To date my greatest bunker shot was hit while I was still an amateur several years ago. I was on the seventeenth hole at the Bass River Golf Club here in South Yarmouth on Cape Cod. Having landed in the rear bunker with the pin cut on the top level or a two tiered green with a descent lie but very little green to work with I laid back the face of my sand wedge wide open. The ball had to go almost straight up in the air and stop quickly near the flag. My sandwedge slipped nicely under the ball causing it to rise up softly and land on the fringe of the green. It then trickled slowly toward the pin, to the edge of the cup; hesitated, and dropped in for a Birdie which closed out my opponent.

At the Green

Here we use the explosion shot, a very unusual shot and an important one. Good execution takes a lot of practice, but this shot can save you a lot of strokes. The trick is to lift the ball out of the sand and place it on the green in good position. A poor shot can leave in the trap, or send the ball flying over the other side of the green. Use your sand wedge and go at it this way:

1. Open your stance and let your arms swing freely in front of your body.

2. Dig your feet into the sand to secure a good footing and get the feel of the sand texture (wet or dry).

3. Open the club face so the grooves point to your left heel. This adds loft and helps get the ball over the lip of the bunker.

4. Pick your spot to hit **behind** the ball and hold your club over that spot. The distance your ball will travel depends on the amount of sand you take. If you are near the pin, the spot you hit will be farther from the ball. For a longer distance, hit closer to the ball, take less sand.

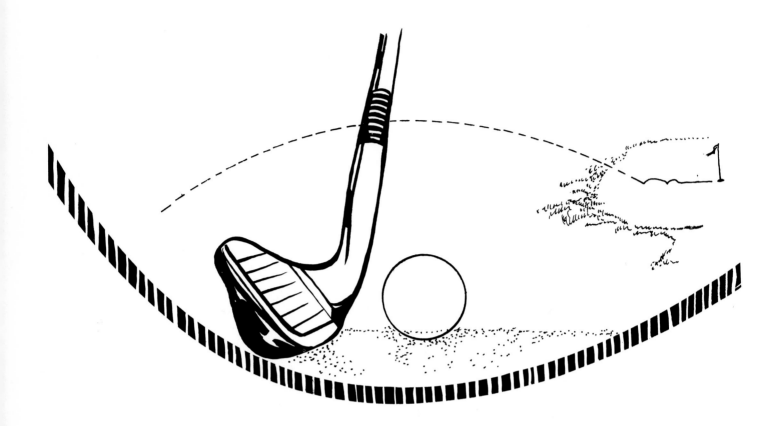

5. The swing in the trap is like a U; on the backswing bring up the club more abruptly, to about shoulder height.

6. On the downswing, you don't strike the ball but the sand behind it. Make sure the clubhead continues on through under the ball and accelerates in a good, high follow-through.

7. A key thought is to hit the flange of the sand wedge against the sand, not the ball, then follow through.

8. Avoid the two most common faults: Not following through, which will leave your ball still in the trap; and hitting the ball instead of the sand.

Hitting the **ball** usually means you overshoot the green or hit the lip and the ball rolls back into the trap. **Hit the sand!**

The Buried Lie
This is called the fried egg because the ball is partly buried and only the top is showing.

1. Take the sand wedge and close the face so the grooves are pointing towards the right foot. This causes more of a digging action to get under the ball.

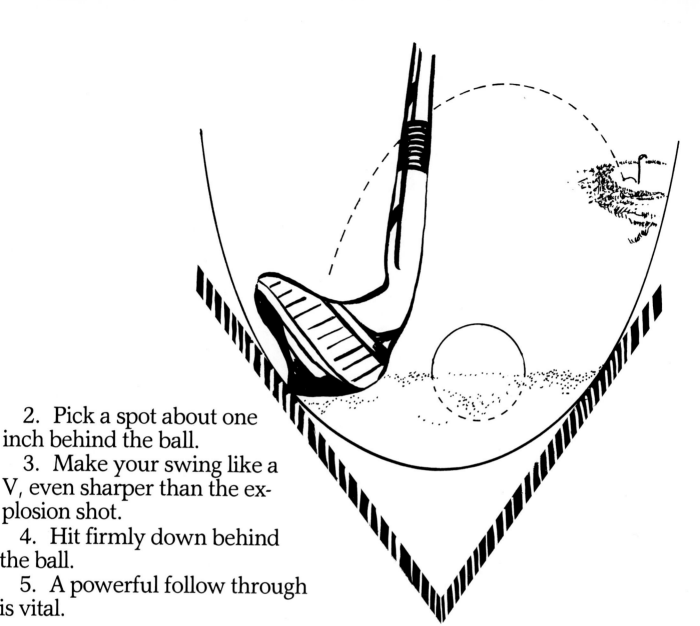

2. Pick a spot about one inch behind the ball.

3. Make your swing like a V, even sharper than the explosion shot.

4. Hit firmly down behind the ball.

5. A powerful follow through is vital.

The Fairway Bunker
These bunkers are usually lower and shallower than the bunkers at the green and thus easier to get out of. From the fairway trap we are trying for much more distance.

1. Use a club with enough loft to get the ball up, this often means a seven wood or five iron, depending on the distance.

2. Plant your feet firmly in the sand for balance.

3. Choke up on the club and use mainly a body swing.

4. Try to pick the ball off the sand. On this spot hit the ball **before** you hit the sand, so as not to deaden the blow to the ball.

5. Swing smooth and don't force it. The ball will usually fly low because your club is hitting the top two-thirds of the ball.

The Water Hole

Getting over the water is mostly in your mind. The carry over the water is usually fairly short, and the shot would normally be a piece of cake, **if the water wasn't there.** So blot out the water from your mind; this is just a normal shot over dry land! And adopt an affirmative attitude! You **can** make the shot, you **will** make the shot. Think positively about where you want to place your ball **beyond** the water, then step up and hit it with confidence.

A friend of mine continually landed in the water whenever it was in his range, causing his fear of the water to increase each time. When he finally came to me with his problem I asked him what he looked at when he had to play over water. "The water," was his answer. I suggested that he focus his attention to a spot OVER the water and visualize his shot flying toward it.

Chapter 12: UNEVEN LIES

Golfing often presents you with challenges, like the uneven lie. These lies require a change in stance and club selection, depending upon the lie.

The Uphill Lie

1. Select a less lofted club than normal as the ball flies higher. If the shot called for a five iron, use a four to achieve the normal ball trajectory.

2. Stand with the ball inside the left heel because the ball is beyond the normal center of the bottom of the swing arc.

3. Lean to the slope, which in this case is forward on the left foot.

4. Avoid the tendency to pull these shots to the left.

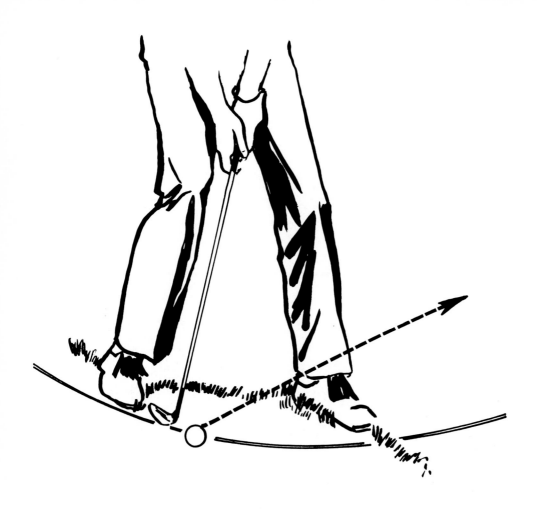

Downhills Lies

This is the most difficult of the uneven lies because the slope is facing downward.

1. Use a much more lofted club than normal. If the shot called for a five iron, use a seven to get the ball up on a normal trajectory.

2. Stand forward, with the ball inside the right heel as you encounter the slope much quicker than normal.

3. Put your weight on the right side to keep your balance down the hill.

Sidehill Lies

The sidehiller is when the ball is above or below the level of your feet. If it is above your feet, center it in your stance and choke up on the club. Select the club next higher to the one you would normally use. Aim slightly to the right, to compensate for the tendency to pull left, and place your weight on your toes.

If the ball is below your feet, center it as above and use a longer-shafted club. Bend from the waist, with your weight on your heels, and aim slightly left of target.

Chapter 13: TROUBLE SHOTS

These are the unusual shots, such as when you have to hook or slice intentionally, or play in heavy wind, or from a bad lie. Knowing how to handle these trouble shots can save you strokes, so let's try a few situations:

The Slice

The slice is a left-to-right shot, and can be useful at times to get out of a tough lie. To get a slice, open and align your stance and shoulders to the left of where you want the ball to go, but open your clubface so it is aimed at the traget. Take a normal swing and the ball will fly higher and drift to the right. If you want more slice, adjust your stance more to the left, keeping the club face pointed at the target.

The Hook

This is the reverse of the slice, that is: working toward the right to make the ball drift left. Once again, keep your club aimed at the target, and if you want more hook turn your body farther right.

Playing the Wind

When playing in the wind, avoid forcing the shot against the wind or on crosswinds. The ability to hit the ball high or low can help you in the wind. It can also help you get the ball back in play from trouble spots like the woods.

Against the Wind

1. Move the ball back 2 or 3 inches in your stance.

2. Choke up on the grip an inch or two.

3. Take a less-lofted club than normal, say a five iron instead of a seven.

4. Shorten up the backswing and follow through; think more of a ¾ swing.

5. Swing easy. A harder swing puts more spin on the ball and sends a bad shot really flying off course.

6. A low trajectory is best, keeping the ball under tree limbs and out of the wind.

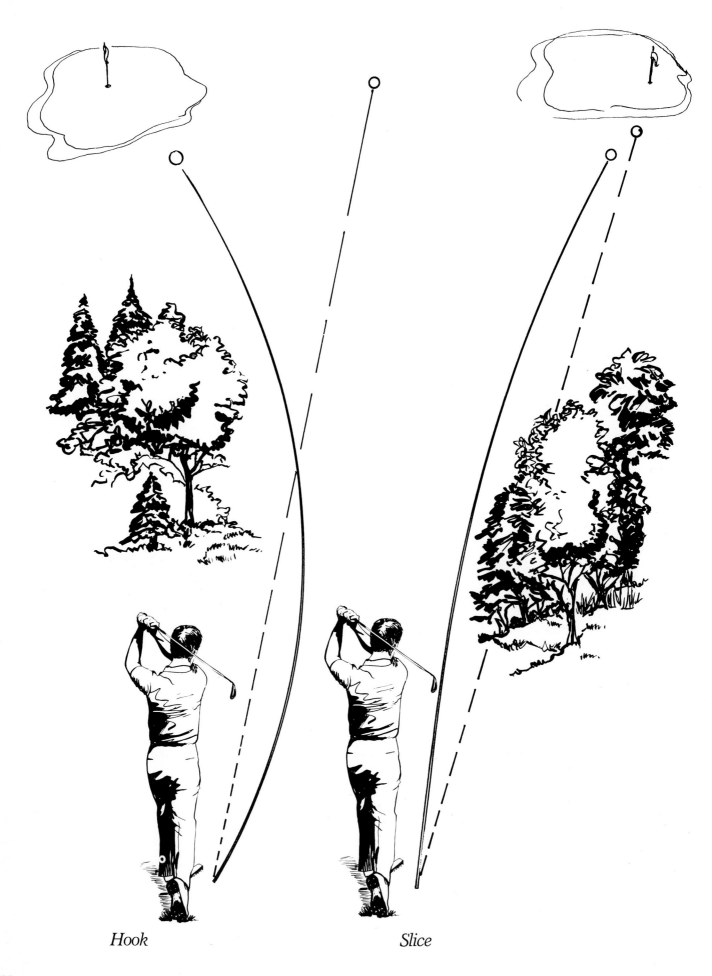

Hook   *Slice*

Downwind Shots

Get the ball flight high to take advantage of the breeze for more distance. Use the wind to get the ball up and over trouble spots and back in play.

1. Move the ball forward in the stance two or three inches left of center.

2. Use a more lofted club. Instead of a five iron use a seven.

3. Attack the ball a little more aggressively downward causing a quicker and higher trajectory.

4. Stay behind the shot longer.

5. Finish high with a good follow-through.

Crosswinds

It is difficult to keep the ball on line in a cross-wind, so you must ride the wind in the direction it's blowing.

1. Address your stance into the direction the wind is blowing from.

2. Hit the shot and let the wind drift it back to the target.

3. Hit the ball firmly. A solidly struck ball will not move off line as much as a poorly hit one.

4. Keep a smooth tempo in your swing.

5. Very rarely give the green away.

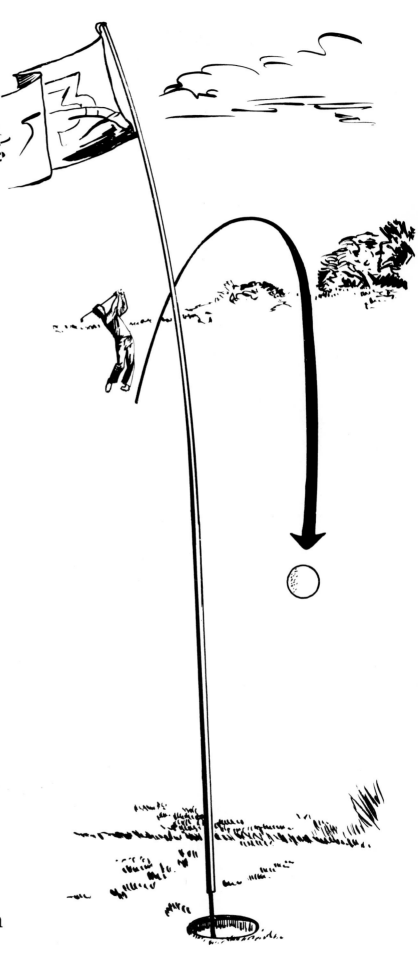

Hitting from a Bad Lie

The most frustrating lie is ending up in another player's divot. This is the best way to get out.

1. Select a more lofted club, usually an iron.
2. Play the ball off the right foot.
3. Keep the hands forward at address.
4. Attack the ball at a steeper angle with a sharp and crisp descending blow to cause the ball to rise.
5. The ball usually comes out lower than normal with a lot of roll.

Cape Cod is shaped like an arm reaching out into the sea. It bends at the "elbow" and then at Provincetown the "hand" is cupped toward the "wrist." With Cape Cod Bay, the Nantucket Sound and the Atlantic surrounding the Cape the wind is almost always a factor; especially on those courses near the shore. On an early spring day in 1983 I was playing a Pro-Am at the Wianno Club which is not a particularly long course but is near the sound and the wind is nearly always a serious factor. That day it was cold and windy, making it difficult to control the ball once it got up very high. After the third hole I decided to use my one iron off the tee to hit a low boring tee shot which would cut the wind. My iron shots to the green had to be kept low to hold their line. At times where normally I'd use a nine iron, I had to choke up on a six or seven iron just to keep it low. I even hit a five iron less than 100 yards just to keep out of the strong wind. Ending up one over par won me the event that day by two shots!

Chapter 14: PRACTICING RIGHT!

Practice is essential to anyone who wishes to improve his golf game. But practicing **right** is also essential. Hitting balls aimlessly is not practice; in fact, it can be harmful if you are just ignoring bad habits.

The place to practice is on the practice tee or green, and you should practice with a purpose. You should have a special shot in mind for every stroke you take, because that is what golf is. In a real game, every stroke presents certain problems and every stroke is different from any other. Every practice shot gives you a chance to solve those problems.

If you practice these strokes, using every good habit you have learned, then you will ingrain your good habits. If something is wrong, seek advice from your pro to correcting your fault. That is the productive way to practice. Accentuate your good points, eliminate the bad ones.

Practice is essential after every lesson, whether it is on the course or on the practice tee or green. It is also smart to practice briefly **before** you step up to play a round of golf. When we go to the first tee without preparation, we sometimes revert to bad old habits, just because they seem more comfortable or natural. What we want to do is first be sure our form is right, then work at it. Developing a repeating swing on the course will certainly lead to lower scores.

Just hitting hundreds of balls on a range, without form or instruction, only deepens problems. We don't want to groove a bad swing into a bad habit; we want to develop the right swing and groove **that** into a **good** habit.

When you are practicing, work on only one thought at a time. Your golf swing lasts only about a second, but it contains a dozen or more thoughts and movement patterns. To practice profitably, work on each of these elements, but one at a time, gradually melding them into a swing that is right for the game, and right for you. That's the swing you want to perfect, and that's the one you want to ingrain.

And here's a couple of don'ts. Don't hit balls off the tee until you are too tired to lift the club. Practice in moderation, and pace yourself as to the number of balls you hit. And don't always play balls from good lies. Hit some of them from bad lies, because all golfers encounter bad lies, and the better you solve **those** problems the better your score. A good expression is: Play like you practice and practice like you play.

Some tips for warm-up time:

1. Do some stretching exercises before any practice or play. This will help you keep fit and also put you in the right frame of mind for golf.

2. Hit a few putts on the practice green, to get the feel for making solid contact with the ball. Try some short ones first, then move out for some long ones, to gauge the speed of the greens.

3. Hit a few chip shots with the 7 or 9 iron, again to feel the solid contact and test the greens.

4. Hit about 30 balls on the practice range, about two or three balls with each club in your bag. This will warm you up for both the irons and woods. The last ball you hit should be with the club you are going to tee off with. Then try to tee off within a short time, say five minutes, before your muscles tighten up again, or you lose the "feel" of your warm-up session.

5. Try for a good, constructive attitude for your first shot off the tee. A good opening shot can set the mental tone for a good round of play. If your first shot is not a good one, all is not lost. Try to figure what went wrong and correct the trouble off the second tee. Many a good round can start with a bad opener. The secret of good golf lies in what the pros call "character." It is **bad fortune** that tests your character, not **good fortune.** Strive to correct your bad fortune, and the good fortune will take care of itself.

6. Analyze your game after every round. How many of my tee shots were in the fairway? How many putts did I take on each green? This analysis will help you recognize where your strengths are, and where the weaknesses are. Now you know the areas of your game that need the most work.

7. Remember: Play like you practice, and practice like you play.

Chapter 15: PLAYING THE COURSE

Playing golf is the same thing every day, right? decidedly wrong! Every round of golf is different, every course is different, and even the same course is different every day, depending on the weather, your attitude, who you are playing with, and a host of other factors.

There are lots of things to remember, but most of them can quickly become second nature, automatic, Here we go:

1. **Check your bag.** Be sure that everything you might want is in your bag, but don't carry anything you don't have to. Some of the things you might want to check: Enough tees, balls, markers, gloves, etc. In other words, equipment. Weather gear - umbrella, rain gear, towel, dry socks, etc.

2. **Study your course.** Even your home course plays differently nearly every day, depending on the weather, mowing, pin placement on the greens, etc. If you are playing the course for the first time, study the scorecard to see what the local rules are, where the water holes and dog-legs are, how long the holes are, the special out-of-bounds areas, etc.

3. **Mental attitude.** This is important, but don't let golf overpower you. Remember, esentially it is a game that should be fun, at the same time helping to keep you fit.

4. The professionals work hard at their golf; they have to, it's money in the pocket for them. You can take time to enjoy the game, enjoy the company of those in your party, and enjoy the surroundings-a park-like setting carefully manicured and maintained. Naturally, you'll want to try for your best shot every time, but don't let a missed putt or an errant drive spoil your day. It is not the end of the world. Try for a better shot the next time. Every swing is a new swing, and you can make it better than the last one.

5. Remember that golf has been played for centuries, and no one has every completely mastered it, and never will. But golf can bring you many pleasures, and memories - the people you've played with, the

courses, the competitiveness, the sport, the relaxation and the challenge. These are the things that keep golf alive, and that you can share, in beautiful surroundings and almost anywhere in the world.

6. **Scoring your best.** Playing a round of golf is done with successive strokes, as few as possible, with a variety of clubs over a beautiful terrain in a felicitous environment. To maneuver a ball only 1.68 inches in diameter over 6,000 yards of water hazards, bunkers, trees and traps, keeping it in bounds, without losing it, occasionally fighting wind and rain, within the rules, is a real challenge, to say the least. Besides all this, golf requires thinking and judgement. And they call this a game? They surely do, and a great one it is.

Here are some things I've learned over the years that may help you.

Select the club that will put the odds in your favor. In sports like baseball, hockey and racquetball, the players react by instinct; in golf, try thinking. Think about the shot you are making, and also about the shot that will follow. Sometimes it is better to surrender a few yards of distance off the tee and keep the ball in play. Great distance is no bargain if you lie behind a tree in the rough.

On Cape Cod, where I play most of my golf, the courses are not particularly long, but the narrow fairways and small greens put a premium on accuracy. I've improved my game over the years by hitting more 3 woods and long irons off the tee. This keeps your ball in the fairway and makes your second shot easier.

Don't take unnecessary chances; they can zoom your score. When you are in the rough, take the shortest and most direct route to get out of trouble. A wise man once said that a forest is 90 percent air and 10 percent trees, but don't believe it in golf. Ninety percent of the time your ball seems to hit the last tree on the long way out. And it always bounces wrong, usually for an extra stroke or two.

Know the rules, especially the unplayable lie rule. It is usually better to give up a stroke than get into deeper trouble. Choose the right alignment. Aim your shot for the largest landing area, and stay away from hazards and boundaries. Aim for the fat part of the green and not necessarily the flag stick, especially when it is tucked behind a trap.

Water hazards are 90 percent mental. Many players focus on the water and do badly. Focus instead on a particular spot **beyond** the water and try to land the ball there. That's the positive approach. Your play on the green is also important. Don't always try for those 40-footers. Settle for getting the ball into that two-foot circle around the cup for a comfortable two putts. You'll get your share of the long ones.

And keep in mind one other fundamental: Golf is a game that you should be enjoying. Are you?

In one of my recent Golf schools at Blue Rock I started out the day with the question, "What percentage of the game do you think is mental?" The replies were from 50% to 99%, and consequently we decided about 80%. Now one might say I need a psychologist rather than a Golf Pro. Let me add that once you've learned to play golf, it's your mental attitude that can make or break your game.

Chapter 16: RULES OF THE GAME

Rules are important in golf, especially in tournament play, amateur or professional. The rules of golf were decodified in 1984 - first comprehensive revision since 1952 - and are now uniform around the world, through the efforts of the United States Golf Association and the Royal and Ancient Golf Club of St. Andrews in Scotland. Anybody can buy a small, handy book of rules for $1 from golf pros, golf shops, or the USGA, Far Hills, New Jersey 07931. There is no excuse for bloodshed on the 19th Hole; all arguments can be settled in a civilized way for $1.

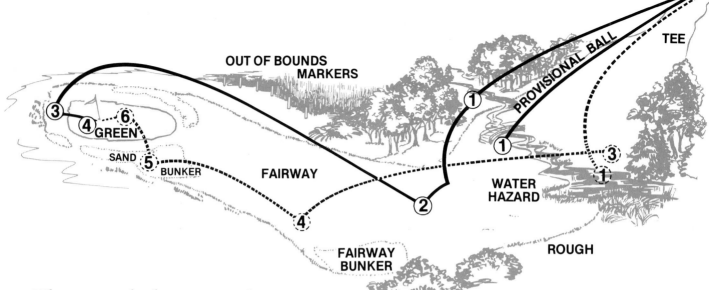

The casual player needs to know the basic rules, and they are simple and sensible, easily learned in routine play. There are a few that apply to most common problems:

1. **Lost ball.** If it is not found in five minutes, replay from the original spot and take a 1-stroke penalty.

2. **Out of bounds,** Replay from the original spot. 1-stroke penalty.

3. **Unplayable lie.** Replay it from the original spot, or drop it within two club lengths of your lie, but in no case any nearer the hole. Take a 1-stroke penalty.

4. **Water hazard.** If you go into the water, replay from original spot. 1-stroke penalty.

5. **Wrong ball.** If you play the wrong ball, replay the correct ball and take a 2-stroke penalty.

6. **Casual water.** If you land in a temporary accumulation of water, snow, or ice, you get a free lift of one club-length.

7. **Flag stick.** It must be removed when you are playing on the green. Hitting it is a 2-stroke penalty.

It is a good idea to know your rule book, to know the difference between match and medal play, and to save strokes. A good knowledge of the rules is essential for competitive play, of course. So get your own rule book and study it at your leisure. You'll understand the game better and enjoy it more.

Chapter 17: THE ETIQUETTE OF GOLF

Golf has always been a game for ladies and gentlemen, and it still is. That's as it should be, because golf is a **social** game, in the best sense of that word. It is enjoyed by civilized and intelligent people who adhere to rules and customs that make the game fair and fun for all.

Be careful of leaving spike marks on the green.

Smooth out your foot prints from bunker.

A common problem is slow play. Golf cannot be played well in a rush, of course, but on a crowded course play should move as quickly as comfortable. Foursomes should be able to play an 18-hole round in four hours if a few simple courtesies are observed.

On the tee, take only one practice swing. Know whose turn it is and be ready to play. Take a couple of clubs with you if you are undecided which one to use, eliminating multiple trips back to your bag. If you are farthest away from the hole, be ready to play first. All of these things can speed play, and are the thoughtful things that make golf the game it is. In the long run they benefit you as well as the other players.

Always enter a sand trap from the lowest area, so as not to break down the edges. Leave the trap the same place you entered it, and smooth out your footprints as you go.

On the green, farthest away plays first. Avoid unnecessary talk or movement while others are putting. Mark your ball and lift it if you are in someone else's way. Short putts can be tapped in to save time. Avoid stepping in the line of play of others, and repair any damage to the green that can affect play. Keep power carts away from the green, and lay the flag stick off to the side; don't throw it.

Leave your bag or cart off the green, in the direction of the next hole. Replace all divots. Let the group behind you play through if you feel you are delaying them. Know what ball you are playing and keep an eye on it; don't play the wrong ball.

These are some of the niceties of golf, and you will pick up others as you play the game. In essence, golf is a game of good manners. Observing the etiquette of golf makes the game more enjoyable for all.

Golf clubs come in many different shapes and forms, and many different prices, but don't be discouraged or dismayed. Golf is basically a simple game of a club hitting a ball, and as a beginner you can join the fun with a few basic clubs and prices and advance as far and as fast as your pocketbook and your desires allow.

For starters, you need only a couple of woods - say a #3 and a #7 - and some basic irons - 3, 5, 7, 9 and a putter. You should be able to get a good quality starter set of clubs for $100 to $150.

One caution:
Men should play only with men's clubs, and women with women's. Women's clubs are shorter, lighter, more flexible and have smaller grips. Your pro can help you choose the best clubs for your play, in upgrading your clubs as you progress in the game, and in selecting special clubs for disabilities.

Working with a golf professional - especially one who is also a clubmaker - can have many advantages. He or she can help you try out various types of clubs, adjust clubs to your needs, and be sure you are getting the advantage of the right club length, degree of flex, shaft material, grip size. For example, seniors often do better with larger grips, to compensate for declining hand strength; or more loft on the clubhead, or the right club sole for your stance.

Selecting Clubs

Regardless of price, all golf clubs have certain characteristics which will be of interest to you. And although all golf clubs may look alike at first glance, you will soon begin to see that there are also many differences, such as price range, design, weight, and materials. As you advance in the game, you will learn enough about clubs to be able to choose the ones that help your game, and that are cost efficient; that is, they produce good results for a reasonable cost. Here are some of the club characteristics you'll be considering.

1. Shaft Length

Club length is determined on individual characterics - the player's height, set-up position, arm length, and the like. Buying clubs is like buying a suit or dress - ready-mades serve adequately for some while others need or prefer tailor-mades. If you have problems, your pro/clubmaker can help in selection and alterations to help your clubs serve your special needs or desires. He or she can also help with guarantees, repairs, and exchanges in clubs.

2. Flex

Shaft flex should be proportionate to the power of the individual's swing. Generally the weaker swinger or older player will benefit from more flex in the shaft.

3. Shaft Material

In the early days of golf, all shafts were made of wood. Then metal shafts came along and today there are a variety of materials. No matter what the shaft is made of, remember that the lighter it is the easier it will be for you to generate clubhead speed, and that means increased distance. The lighter shafts also give you more control, and thus more accuracy.

4. Grip

Grips come in different sizes, just as gloves do. Generally speaking, the smaller the hands, the smaller the grip; conversely, larger hands, larger grip. You can also choose between rubber, cord, and leather grips, though the usually means more expensive clubs.

5. Clubhead Design and Materials

This is important, not only in playing results but in price. Generally speaking, you should look for low profile heads. I prefer more club weight below the center of the ball because it gives more loft and distance.

6. Swingweight

What this means is that all the clubs in a set have the same characteristics of construction and design, resulting in a certain balance or "feel." The swingweight of different sets will vary on the basis of their design and construction. Sets are different because players are different. The set that is best for you will be the one that best fits your particular physical characteristics. The swingweight will be right and so will the "feel."

Caring for Your Clubs

Every good workman knows that he should keep his tools in top condition; the same goes for the golfer. It makes good sense to buy good clubs, and to keep them in top condition. Here are some pointers.

1. Woods

Moisture is the worst enemy; it adds weight to the clubheads and causes warping and swelling. So dry your woods with a towel before you put them away. Store your clubs in a dry area in a moderate temperature. The trunk of your car is **NOT** a good place; it is fequently damp and very hot or cold. Using head covers on your woods is a good idea. This keeps them from banging against the irons and marring or damaging the heads.

2. Irons

Here again, dry the clubs to prevent rust. Clean the gooves with a hard-bristle brush. If you like, you can buff up stainless heads on a soft wheel.

3. The Grip

Grips get oily and dirty during play from the perspiration in your hands. Keep them clean for a better grip and better shots. Wipe down your grips after play. This will prevent mildew and moisture build-up and reduce cracking or slippage in your hand. Don't leave grips exposed to extreme heat or sun. Rubber grips can be cleaned with a Brillo pad warm water; then rinse and wipe dry. This should be done every couple of months. Leather grips should be treated two or three times a year with a leather conditioner, available at pro shops or shoe shops. Leather is harder to maintain than rubber because it dries out quickly if not treated and becomes slippery. The leather should have a tacky feel.

Good preventive care can protect the money you've invested in your clubs. A few minutes of attention will pay off, just as good car care pays off. And remember, clubs can be refinished and provided with new grips at a fraction of the cost of new clubs. In this way, your favorite clubs can stay with you for years.

A few last words about your clubs. As your game develops you are going to be carrying more clubs. The basic set will begin to grow when you add a couple of more woods, like the 1 and 5. In the irons, you'll begin to find a gap between 5 and 7; it's the time to think about adding the 6 iron. In the sand game, you'll begin to look at the wedges for those special shots that can keep your score down.

How many clubs should you have, and how much should you pay?

Those are personal decisions you must make for yourself, just like selecting a car, where you can range from compact to Cadillac. Get the clubs you want and can afford, and be sure to get the **quality you are paying for.** And let your pro help you, just as you rely on professionals in many other decisions of life.

Chapter 19: STAYING IN SHAPE

Staying in shape physically is good for you, and will improve your golf game. The best plan is to schedule a short period of exercise EVERY DAY, whether or not you are going on the course. Simple exercises are the best; they require little or no equipment, and can be done indoors or out, regardless of the weather.

Here are some tips to fitness that are especially keyed to the game of golf:

1. **Legs**. Strong legs are the key to golf, not only for the walking involved but for a strong, effective golf swing. Strong legs will prevent fatigue on the course and encourage you to play more often.

Besides the walking in golf, do lots of walking whenever possible. Walking in sand, such as on the beach, is especially helpful in muscle development and toning. For indoor exercise,

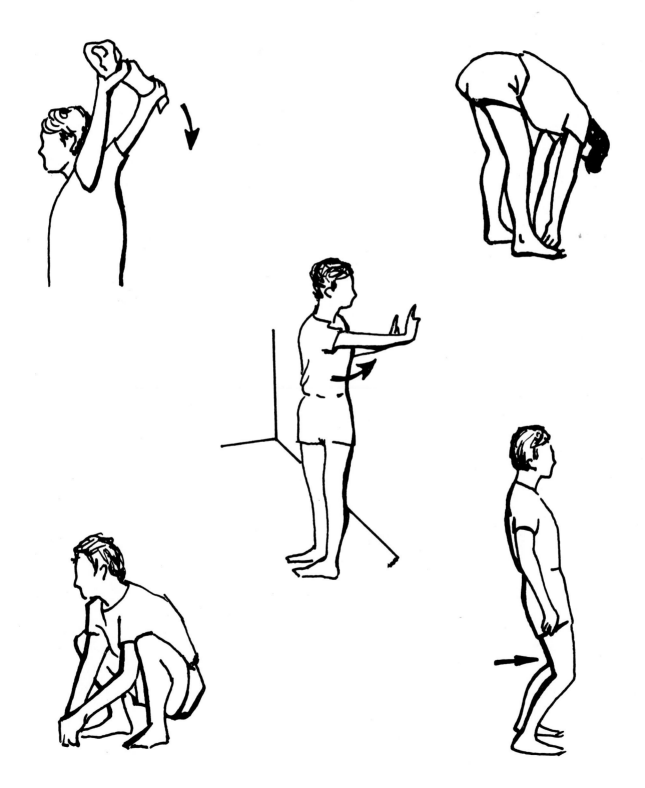

use a stationary bicycle or rowing machine if available to you. Regular exercise at a health club, under professional supervision, is an excellent way to keep your whole body, including the legs, in good condition.

2. **Arms**. You'll feel better, and play better golf, with strong hands, wrists, and forearms. These muscle systems can be kept in condition with simple exercises. For hand development, practice squeezing with a rubber ball or other small, elastic objects. To strengthen your wrists and forearms, practice regularly

Chapter 20: ENJOYING GOLF

With all this attention to learning the game, don't overlook the most important thing in golf — enjoying the game!

Golf is an ageless game; you can come to it at any stage of life. If you come to golf at mid-life or later — and more people are now doing this than ever before — you can look forward to many years of healthful and happy golf. And if you join the world of Senior Golf you will find that it is truly a world experience. You can now combine golf and travel, be it the United States or the world.

Golf is played nearly everywhere in the free world, and you will find the travel and sports establishments happy to meet your desires. There are now senior golf groups, tournaments, tours, and trips ready to take you as far as you like in the world of golf.

And wherever you golf, you will find the social amenities that brought you to the game in the first place. For all its many years, golf remains as much a game of the mind and spirit as of the body. It is a game to be played by gentlemen and gentlewomen the world over, a game of personal challenge that lasts far longer than the time it takes to play a round. Golf goes with you wherever you are, for it is both a game of play and a game of memory.

What better way to have fun and keep fit! Enjoy golf!

GOLF TERMS

Addressing the ball. Taking a stance and grounding the club (except in a hazard) before taking a swing.

Approach. A shot to the putting green.

Apron. Grass area (fringe) immediately surrounding the putting surface.

Away. Ball furthest from the hole; to be played first.

Birdie. One stroke under the designated par of a hole.

Bogey. Usually one stroke over the designated par of a hole.

Bunker. A hazard, often a depression, and usually covered with sand (frequently referred to as a **sand trap**). Grass bordering or within a bunker is *not* considered part of the hazard.

Casual Water. A temporary water accumulation not intended as a hazard.

Divot. Turf displaced by player's club when making a swing.

Dog-leg. A hole in which the route of play angles to the right or left before reaching the putting surface.

Down. The number of holes (match play) or strokes (stroke play) a player is behind an opponent.

Eagle. Two strokes under par for a hole.

Fairway. Closely mowed route of play between teeing area and putting green.

Flagstick. A thin, movable pole with a flag attached at the top, centered in the hole of the putting green to indicate its location. Also called **pin.**

Fore. A warning cry to any person in the way of play.

Forecaddie. A person assigned to indicate to players the positions of balls on the course.

Green. The putting surface.

Gross score. Total number of strokes taken to complete a designated round.

Ground. Touching the surface or ground with the sole of the club at address.

Handicap. A deduction from a player's gross score devised to match his score against par and to equate differential abilities of other players.

Halved. Competitive term used to indicate identical scores on a hole.

Hazard. A term used to designate bunkers (sand traps) or water areas.

Honor. The right to tee off first, earned by scoring lowest on preceding hole.

Hook. A stroke made by a right-handed player which curves the ball to the left of the target. For the left-handed player, the ball will curve to the right.

Hosel. Extension of the club-head into which the hsaft fits.

Lie. Stationary position of the ball in the grass or sand; also, the angle of the shaft in relation to the ground when the club sole rests naturally.

Loose impediment. A natural object, not stationary, growing or adhering to the ball, such as a leaf, twig, branch or the like.

Marker. A person who keeps score. **Tee markers** define the forward limits of the teeing area.

Match play. Type of competition in which each hole is a separate contest. The winner is the player or side that wins more holes than there are left to play.

Nassau. Competition either match or stroke play which awards 1 point for front nine; 1 point for back nine; and 1 point for total 18 holes.

Net score. Gross score, less handicap.

Obstruction. In general, an artificial object erected, placed or left on the course.

Par. A numerical standard of scoring excellence per hole, based on yardage and two putts per green.

Provisional ball. A second ball hit before a player goes to look for his original ball which apparently is out-of-bounds or lost outside a water hazard.

Pull. A straight shot in which the flight of the ball is left of target. For a left-handed player, the flight is right of the target.

Push. A straight shot in which the flight of the ball is right of the target. For a left-handed player the flight is left of the target.

Rough. Areas, usually of relatively long grass, adjacent to the tee, fairway, green or hazards.

Slice. A stroke made by a right-handed player which curves the ball to the right of the intended target. For a left-handed player, the ball will curve to the left.

Stance. Position of the feet when addressing the ball.

Stroke. Any forward motion of the clubhead made with intent to strike the ball.

Stroke play. Competition based on total number of strokes taken.

Target. The spot or area to which the ball is intended to land or roll.

Tee. A peg, or top of which the ball is placed before striking it from the teeing area. Also, the teeing area itself.

Up. The number of holes (match play) or strokes (stroke play) a player leads his opponent.

Blue Rock Golf Course
Tenth Hole
153 yards across the water to an elevated green with two intimidating bunkers.